CHAMPIONS OF FREEDOM AND SELF RELIANCE

The Source for Freedom and Self-Reliant Information[1]

Thomas Jefferson defined *rightful liberty* as "unobstructed action according to our will within limits drawn around us by the equal rights of others—I do not add 'within the limits of the law,' because law is often but the tyrant's will, and always so when it violates the right of an individual."

Unlock the 4-Doors to Financial Independence

By

Robert G. Beard, Jr., C.P.A., C.G.M.A., J.D., LL.M.

---

[1] Each Jeffersonian Group, LLC (www.jeffersoniangroup.com) publication is intended solely for information purposes and is not intended nor does it purport to provide legal, tax, individual investment advice, estate planning advice, insurance advice or business advice. In addition, information and analysis is compiled from sources believed to be reliable but such accuracy cannot be guaranteed. Readers should do their own research and consult with expert legal, tax, insurance, business and financial counsel before taking any action. Copyright © 2018 Jeffersonian Group, LLC

Contents

I. Introduction 1

II. The Key to Door 1 – Pay Yourself First 9

III. The Key to Door 2 – Live Below Your Means 12

IV. The Key to Door 3 – Take Advantage of the Greatest Opportunity to Come Around in Our Lifetime 17

    A. How I Bought Stellar Lumens (XLM) 19

    B. Tax Consequences of Speculating in Bitcoin and Other Crypto-Currencies 23

    C. Final Thoughts 25

V. The Key to Door 4 – Invest in DRIP's 26

    A. It's Never Too Late 30

    B. How to Use DRIP's to Attain and Maintain Financial Freedom 32

        i. Why Invest in Specific Stocks That Pay Dividends? 32

        ii. How to Select DRIP Stocks 36

        iii. Basic Portfolio 37

        iv. Other U.S. Dividend Champions to Consider 44

        v. Contenders Worthy of Consideration 45

        vi. Challengers You May Want to Consider 46

        vii. How to Begin Investing 47

        viii. Diversification Myths and What Not to Buy 48

VI. Wrapping It All Up 52

About the Author 55

Other Publications 55

I. Introduction

How would you like to become wealthy and financially independent? If you have obtained financial independence, how would you like to maintain your financial freedom? How would you like to see your children and grandchildren obtain financial independence early in their lives no matter what job or career they choose; and, no matter how many mistakes they make along the way? And finally, how would you like to see your parents retire without worrying about outliving their money? If you answered yes to any one of these questions, then you have come to the right place!

With over 40-years working as a *Certified Public Accountant* helping people start and run businesses, protect their assets, and plan for their retirement, I have seen what works and what does not. In today's ever-changing world, when it comes to investing, the typical advice received from the financial planning community may inhibit your ability to attain financial freedom; and, cause many of you to outlive your money in your retirement years. There are several authors that agree with me.

For example, Ben Stein wrote a book entitled, *How To Really Ruin Your Financial Life And Portfolio*. Stein was enamored with Warren Buffet and his company Berkshire Hathaway (BRK), which became successful by investing in great businesses that pay dividends but, has never paid a dividend to his stockholders. Stein concluded that the typical investor is better off investing in low-cost index funds and avoiding the advice of brokers, money managers, and Wall Street in general. Although Stein mentioned the benefit of reinvesting dividends, it appeared to be an after-thought; he never mentioned that there are over 100 companies, *U.S. Dividend Champions*, that have paid and raised their annual dividends each, and every year, for 25 or more years in a row; or, that there are many *Contenders* that have paid and raised dividends for 10-to-24 years in a row. If he had known about these companies and their dividend reinvestment programs, he would have been remiss by not including this information in his book.

Why would Stein not know about these programs? Because Wall Street cannot make any money from them. Furthermore, the SEC, influenced by the power-brokers on Wall Street, have forbidden these companies from advertising their programs; and, if the average investor stumbles across them, the companies are required to send them a huge prospectus—most likely requiring an attorney or an accountant to interpret—outlining the risks and none of the benefits of their programs.

In 2017, Tony Robbins came out with a book titled, *Unshakeable, Your Financial Freedom Playbook, Creating Peace of Mind in a World of Volatility*. Robbins interviewed many of the *Titans of Wall Street*, e.g., Warren Buffet, John Bogle (founder of Vanguard Mutual Funds), and Peter Mallouk, co-author and "Wealth Advisor."

Robbins makes a great argument for investing in the stock market, but, not by buying actively managed mutual funds. John Bogle, the founder of Vanguard Mutual Funds, wrote the forward and stated:

…index fund investors receive the gross market return minus fees as low as 0.05%…while active investors as a group will receive the same gross return minus 2% or more…

Over an investment lifetime, this annual difference [in fees] really adds up. Most young people just starting their careers will be investing for 60 years or more. **Compounded over that time frame, the high costs of investing can confiscate an astounding 70% of your lifetime returns!**…

But we don't have to put up 100% of the capital and take 100% of the risk only to receive 30% of the reward (often far less). By buying low-cost, broad-market index funds (and holding them "forever"), you can guarantee that you will receive your fair share of whatever returns the financial markets provide over the long term.

Robbins rightly concluded,

The problem is, most funds do a terrific job of charging high fees but a terrible job of picking successful investments. One study showed that 96% of mutual funds failed to beat the market over a 15-year period. The result? You overpay for underperformance. It's like paying for a Ferrari and then driving home from the dealership in a beaten-up tractor splattered with mud.

Even worse, those fees add up massively over time. **If you overpay by 1% a year, it will cost you 10 years' worth of retirement income.**[2]

Like Ben Stein, Tony Robbins did not allude to the existence of the *U.S. Dividend Champions* and *Contenders*. He interviewed the *Titans of Wall Street*[3] to come up with his recommendations. Most of them made their fortunes by selling investment products to the average investor.

---

[2] "This assumes two investors with a starting investment of $100,000, equal returns of 8% over 30 years, but with 1% fees and 2% fees, respectively. Assuming an equal withdrawal amount at retirement, the investor paying 2% in fees will run out of money 10 years sooner." **It is interesting that Robbin's co-author, Peter Mallouk most likely charges 1% for his financial planning and investment advice** and this book is promoting his services, along with Tony Robbins Companies. **My advice: Save another 1% and another 10 years of retirement income by investing in DRIP's!** By investing in DRIP's you will most likely not have to touch your principal; only the dividend payments which increase by 10% or more each and every year. **This DRIP strategy,** *which you can implement yourself,* **will be explained in more detail throughout this book.**

[3] T. Boone Pickens, Kyle Bass, Charles Schwab, Sir John Templeton, Carl Icahn, Robert Schiller, Dan Ariely, Burton Malkiel, Marc Faber, Warren Buffet, John Bogle, Ray Dalio, Alan Greenspan, Steve Forbes, etc.

Robbins made investing more complicated than it should be and promoted the services of his co-author, Peter Mallouk, who most likely charges 1% annually of your investment capital for his services. Robbins was, and probably still is, on the Board and Chief of Investor Psychology for Creative Planning, Inc. for which he received, and will most likely continue to receive, compensation. Therefore, Robbins would not benefit if he identified and provided an alternative to seeking the advice of his financial planning company. However, it is highly likely that he was unaware of the benefits of investing in certain companies that have dividend reinvestment programs (DRIP's). After all, practically every expert he interviewed made their money by selling products developed by Wall Street. DRIP's were not even a topic for consideration.

If you were unaware of DRIP's and you finished Robbin's book, you would probably be convinced that your only alternative to *financial freedom* is to seek out the services of Robbins and Mallouk's companies. After all, Robbins suggested that you do need help when it comes to financial planning; and, that Creative Planning, Inc., his company, is one of a limited number of financial planning firms that would look out for your interests, not theirs. **Rubbish...** Tony Robbin's book is an advertisement for his services, which you will not need, nor any other financial advisor or money manager!

After reading **this** book, you may be able to save substantial fees and obtain financial freedom much earlier by taking control of your own financial affairs and not relying on an entire industry designed to sell you investment products. **It does not matter if you make $25,000 a year or $1,000,000 or more per year** and **it does not matter if you are 18 years old or 70 years old.**

KEEP READING!

When I was with a certain "Big 8"—now the Big 4, due to mergers—international public accounting firm, an old joke by one of our investment banking clients went like this: If the broker and syndicator makes money, 2 out of 3 ain't bad. Many times, the unsuspecting investors, who put up all the money would break-even or lose much of their investment capital, while the brokers and syndicators made money upfront, risking nothing if the investment failed. If the investment was a success, the broker-dealer and syndicator reaped the most profit while the investors, who took all the risk ended up with an average return; many times, a below average return.

Ben Stein, Tony Robbins, and John Bogle, founder of Vanguard, all agreed that mutual fund and advisory fees can easily "cost you [at least] 10 years' worth of retirement income." As Rick Ferri wrote, Forbes Personal Finance, May 27, 2013, "The thought of giving up 40% per year in investment return to pay for portfolio management and advice would cause most people to walk away." Unfortunately, many investors have no idea that they are paying upwards of 40% of their return each year in fees; and, the people who understand this, believe they have no alternative.

But, there is an alternative to avoid all fees. You can invest directly in great businesses—that have survived wars, recessions, and depressions—that have paid and raised their annual dividends each and every year for 25-years and longer. For example, The Coca-Cola Company (KO) has paid and raised its annual dividend each and every year for the past 55-years. Its name or brand is one of the most recognized throughout the world, selling its products in over 200 countries. If you had purchased 100 shares of KO on November 30, 1994 for $5,112 using the Company's DRIP or dividend reinvestment program, after 18 years ending December 17, 2012, your 100 shares would have grown to 1,958 shares worth $73,914 representing an average annual return per year of 74.56%. More importantly, the dividend yield, at the time of purchase was only 1.5% or $78. For the year ended December 17, 2012, that dividend payout to you would have grown to $1,977.44 representing a one-time yield or return on your original investment, just from the dividends received, for the year

2012 of 38.68%; this annual yield continues to increase each and every year. For the year ending December 15, 2016, the last quarterly dividend payment in 2016, the total dividends paid was $3,053.46 on this original investment of $5,112 representing a total return for 2016 of 59.73% based upon the dividend payments alone. And, within several more years, the annual dividend payments will exceed the original investment!

By investing in DRIP's, sponsored by great businesses like The Coca-Cola Company (KO), **you are able to take advantage of the miracle of compound interest,** with all of your money going into the investment; and, none of your money is siphoned-off by brokers, money managers, and financial planners.

According to Einstein, "compound interest is the eighth wonder of the world. He who understands it, earns it...he who doesn't...pays it." By investing in great businesses—that have survived recessions, depressions, and wars—with dividend reinvestment programs (DRIP's), that pay a certain yield when purchased and that have paid and raised their annual dividend payments each and every year for 25-years or more, you are able to take advantage of the laws of compound interest, "the eighth wonder of the world!"

In addition to the real-life Coca-Cola (KO) example mentioned above, look at the story of three hardworking self-reliant Americans, who also benefited from the miracle of compound interest:

(1) Grace Groner graduated from Lake Forest College in 1931 and went to work as a secretary at Abbott Laboratories. In 1935, she invested $180 in three shares of Abbott Laboratories (ABT) and reinvested the dividends for the next 75 years. When she died in 2010, her $180 original investment was worth $7-million due to stock splits and reinvested dividends.

(2) Anne Scheiber, who worked as an IRS Auditor for 23 years turned

a $5,000 investment made in 1944 into $22-million by the time she passed away in 1995 at the age of 101. She acquired stocks of companies like Coca-Cola (KO) and reinvested the dividends for decades.

(3) Ronald Read, a World War II veteran with a high school education, worked as a gas station attendant for 25 years, then as a janitor for 17 more years before retiring at the age of 76. When he passed away at age 92 in 2014, he had a portfolio of great businesses (e.g., Johnson & Johnson, Procter & Gamble, Colgate-Palmolive) worth $8-million by reinvesting the dividends.

Investing in great businesses that have paid and raised dividends for decades is not written about much in the mainstream financial media. Wall Street cannot make money by publicizing these DRIP's, which ordinary investors can acquire on their own. Wall Street makes billions in commissions selling mutual funds, annuities, and other financial products that are not necessarily in the best interests of investors.

Included within this book is an approach to investing that is supported by several professors in academia. According to Dr. Jeremy Siegel, a professor of finance at the prestigious Wharton School of Business, "The evidence is overwhelming that dividend-paying stocks are still your best long-term investment." Louisiana State University professors Harvey Rubin and Carlos Spaht, II concluded in several of their studies,

the case for the long-term dividend investment strategy will lead to financial independence for life. Regardless of the direction of the market, a constant and growing dividend is a never-ending income stream.

...financial independence for life can be achieved with relatively small sums of money by making quality dividend investments and being disciplined to do the same thing period after period of time.

Based on over 40-years of experience, investing in certain DRIP's is the only long-term investment strategy that consistently provides an ever-increasing dividend or annual cash-flow, regardless of whether the stock market rises or falls. Think about it, why do we work? To create a cash flow that maintains our lifestyle. **I will show you how to create a cash flow so you no longer have to work to support yourself and your family.**

However, **there are two other things you must consistently do; and, a once in a lifetime opportunity, that may only last several years**, that just might lead to financial independence much sooner than expected. Even if you are unsuccessful with this once in a lifetime opportunity, you will still be able to obtain financial independence within 10-to-15 years.

My objective with this book is to provide you with the tools necessary to take care of your own financial affairs; to help you steer clear of the sharks on Wall Street; to outlive your money; to attain financial independence as soon as possible; and, to maintain your financial freedom regardless of what is happening in the markets and the world. Or, as the late Harry Browne wrote, *How to Live Free in an Unfree World*.

KEEP READING... I'll give you the four Keys to unlock the Doors to Financial Independence!

II. The Key to Door 1 – Pay Yourself First

Financial Independence has nothing to do with your net worth (assets less liabilities). There are many millionaires who are not financially independent; if they lost their 6-to-7 figure incomes from their jobs or career, many would have to file for bankruptcy. Many millionaires work every day to pay their mortgages on several homes, yachts, and all of their other expensive trappings of perceived wealth; they are slaves of the banks, who they pay their mortgages to; they are slaves of government who they pay their federal & state income taxes, Medicare & Social Security Taxes, and the ever-increasing real estate taxes on their lavish homes. If they must work at their jobs and careers to maintain their lifestyle, they are not financially independent.

Real wealth is a cash flow generated from your passive investments or assets that exceeds your expenses necessary to support the lifestyle of your choosing. You do not have to go to work; you may wake up at 6:00 am or noon; you may travel and live anywhere; and, your passive income or cash flow continues to flow into your bank account 24/7 regardless of whether you are awake, or asleep.

Once you become financially independent, you may choose to continue working; you may start another career or business; you may decide to go back to school; you may start a charitable foundation; or, you might just want to do nothing but travel and see the world. Once you have obtained financial freedom, you are no longer a slave and can do whatever you want; the choice is yours!

To become financially independent, **the first key necessary to unlock Door 1 is to Pay Yourself First**; if you are already financially independent, you must continue using this key!

A common strategy recommended by financial planners is to take the first 10% of your earnings and put it into your savings, which has now been coined, the pay-yourself-first principle. For example, when you sit down to pay your bills or common living expenses (e.g., rent or mortgage, utilities, auto, etc.) the first payment should be to yourself. Normally it is recommended that you take the first 10% of your earnings or paycheck and save or invest that amount every time you pay your bills. The 10% should be based upon your gross salary or earnings, not the net amount, which is after withholding for federal income taxes, State & local taxes, Social Security & Medicare taxes.

In today's uncertain world, when job security is no longer the norm, 10% may not be enough. You should attempt to save and invest at least 30% of your gross salary or earned income. If you make a habit of this and live below your means, it will become second nature.

Parents and grandparents can help their children and grandchildren learn this valuable lesson when they receive cash money for doing chores or working, or, for birthdays and other holidays. For example, if your child receives $10, have them put $3 in a piggybank or savings jar. The goal is to accumulate at least $600 to be able to open an account with an online discount broker. If they receive $1,000 from generous grandparents for a birthday, take at least $600 and open a brokerage account with an online discount broker and show them how to buy 10 shares of Coca-Cola (KO) stock. Explain to them that The Coca-Cola Company has over 500 sparkling and still brands selling 1.9-billion servings per day in over 200 countries. And, every time we drink a bottle of Dasani purified water, or any other Coke products you may like to drink, we, as owners of this great business, are helping to make our stock more valuable; and, enable our company to continue to pay and raise its dividends, which is good for us and the entire economy of the United States.

As will be explained and demonstrated throughout this book, the sooner one starts to invest using the principle of compound interest, by buying great businesses—that have survived recessions, depressions and wars—that have paid and raised their annual dividends for at least 25 years and longer, the sooner one is able to attain financial freedom.

However, to be able to invest in these great businesses, **you must continually Pay Yourself First throughout your entire life.**

III. The Key to Door 2 – Live Below Your Means

To be financially independent and maintain your financial freedom, you must accumulate assets or investments that pay you passive income that continues to grow and is always greater than your expenses necessary to maintain your lifestyle. If you are creative and able to develop a product or fill a need, purchase the next Bitcoin, or, be lucky enough to win a lottery and generate millions-of-dollars, you may be temporarily financially independent. But, if you want to maintain your financial freedom, you will need to acquire assets or investments that pay you passive income that continues to grow and is always greater than your expenses to maintain your lifestyle.

Unfortunately, anywhere from 44%-to-70% of lottery winners and others that receive a windfall end up broke within five years because they do not understand this principle. **To maintain financial freedom, you must acquire assets or investments that generate passive income that continues to grow; and, your passive income must always exceed the expenses necessary to maintain your lifestyle.** If you have to liquidate or sell your investments to maintain your lifestyle, you will ultimately run out of money, which is what happens to most lottery winners.

For most of us, the greatest amount of income or cash flow that we receive comes from our jobs or careers, whether we work for others or ourselves. Therefore, you should first do all that you can to maximize your job or career earnings. If you are unhappy with your career choice or you cannot generate enough income from your chosen career, try something else.

My grandfather, a World War I veteran, self-educated, and who built bridges in Northern Illinois and Wisconsin while employing many others during the depression-era, advised: Look at every job as a paid education; once you have learned all you can from a particular job, move on to another job until you have learned and saved enough to start your own business. So, if you are unhappy with your current employment, take my grandfather's advice, i.e., look at your current position as a paid education, work another part-time job to enhance your education, find another job to continue your paid education, and then, start your own business to increase your income.

Unfortunately, since the industrial revolution, our government-controlled schools no longer encourage the entrepreneurial and independent spirit. The U.S. education system was designed, based upon the German-system;[4] to stifle individual intuitive; to encourage students to be satisfied with mundane factory-type jobs (or today, work 8-to-10 hours a day at a desk in an administrative position); to follow orders; and, to respect authority and pay their taxes to the federal government without question. And, the easiest way for the U.S. government to collect taxes is for most citizens to be employed by companies that withhold and deposit taxes directly to the Internal Revenue Service.[5] While the entrepreneur and self-employed tend to be more creative, taking advantage of available loopholes in the tax laws.

Many people are "highly-educated, professionally successful, and financially illiterate."[6] This is due to our compulsory education or indoctrination system,[7] which encourages like-minded thinking, finding a

---

[4] "The structure of American schooling...began in 1806 when Napoleon's amateur soldiers beat the professional soldiers of Prussia at the battle of Jena." As a result, in 1819 compulsory schooling began for the Prussian people with "a clear vision" to deliver: "1) Obedient soldiers to the army; 2) Obedient workers to the mines; 3) Well subordinated civil servants to government; 4) Well subordinated clerks to industry; 5) Citizens who thought alike about major issues. Privacy Alert, the Suprynowicz Letter, Vol. III, No. 8 (October 2003). Also see John Taylor Gatto, *The Underground History of American Education, An Intimate Investigation Into the Prison of Modern Schooling*, Oxford Village Press (2006).

[5] This system of payroll withholding was established in 1943 during World War II when the United States needed more money to fund the war effort.

[6] Robert T. Kiyosaki, *Rich Dad Poor Dad*, 79, Plata Publishing, LLC (April 2017).

[7] See John Taylor Gatto, *The Underground History of American Education, An Intimate Investigation Into the Prison of Modern Schooling*, Oxford Village Press (2006).

good paying job, and reliance on government to solve all problems. As a result, most people become "trapped in the Rat Race."[8] Robert Kiyosaki illustrated how a financial dream turns into a financial nightmare:

> The classic story of hardworking people has a set pattern. Recently married, the happy, highly educated young couple now share a cramped rented apartment. Immediately, they realize that they are saving money because two can live as cheaply as one.
>
> The problem is the apartment is cramped. They decide to save money to buy their dream home so they can have kids. They now have two incomes, and they begin to focus on their careers. Their incomes begin to increase.
>
> ...as a result of their incomes increasing, they decide to buy the house of their dreams. Once in their house with a mortgage, they have a new tax, called property tax. Then they buy a new car, new furniture, and new appliances to match their new house. All of a sudden they wake up and their liabilities column is full of mortgage and credit card debt.
>
> Their liabilities go up.
>
> They're now trapped in the Rat Race. Pretty soon a baby comes along and they work harder. The process repeats itself: Higher incomes cause higher taxes, also called "bracket creep." A credit card comes in the mail. They use it and max it out. A loan company calls and says their greatest "asset," their home, has appreciated in value. Because their credit is so good, the company offers a bill-consolidation loan and tells them the intelligent thing to do is clear off the high-interest consumer debt by paying off their credit card. And besides, mortgage interest is a tax

---

[8] Kiyosaki, *supra* note 6 at 78.

deduction. They go for it and pay off those high-interest credit cards. They breathe a sigh of relief. Their credit cards are paid off. They've now folded their consumer debt into their home mortgage. Their payments go down because they extend their debt over 30 years. It is the smart thing to do.

Their neighbor calls to invite them to go shopping. The Memorial Day sale is on. They promise themselves they'll just window shop, but they take a credit card, just in case.[9]

As Kiyosaki correctly explained, the problem the typical hard-working couple has is not how to make more money but, "their trouble is really how they choose to spend the money they have." "It is caused by financial illiteracy and not understanding the difference between an asset and a liability."[10]

Contrary to popular opinion, a home is not an asset for creating real wealth, it is a liability.[11] Your home does not generate any income; it is a *Money Pit*. You must pay the mortgage, utilities, maintenance, property taxes that continue to go up each year, and, insurance that tends to also increase annually. After so many years, kitchens need remodeling, carpets & flooring replaced, and, painting and decorating requiring new furniture to match the updated changes. And, the larger the home the more furniture that is needed to fill it up.

To become financially independent, you need to keep your expenses low, limit or eliminate your liabilities, and, accumulate assets or investments that pay you an income. You must keep your expenses low so that you have enough income to acquire assets or investments on a regular basis. The earlier you start, the sooner you will become financially independent.

---

[9] *Id.* at 75-78.

[10] *Id.* at 78.

[11] *Id.* at 83.

For those of you who have just left college or a trade school and have landed a new job or career near your parents, consider moving back home to save on rent, utilities, etc., which may enable you to save 30%-to-50% or more of your gross earnings over a one-to-two-year period. You might also consider sharing an apartment or rental house with several roommates to keep your living expenses low.

If you move into a neighborhood where everybody drives luxury cars and belong to country clubs, you will most likely end up making the same choices as your neighbors. However, if you curtail your immediate desires for gratification and acquire assets that generate passive income, you will become financially independent much sooner.

To become financially independent and maintain your financial freedom, you must always live below your means, i.e., your income must always exceed your expenses necessary to maintain your lifestyle. Whatever your income is, you should be able to save and invest 10%-to-30% of it. For example, if your monthly income is $5,000, you should be able to invest 10% of that amount or $500 each month; if $10,000 per month, you should be investing 30% or $3,000; and, if $25,000 per month, you should be investing at least 30% or $7,500 per month. Any bonuses and pay raises should be invested rather than spent on luxuries or to buy a bigger home. Buy that bigger fancier new house after you have accumulated enough assets or investments that generate an increasing passive income that can pay for it.

Married couples who both work should attempt to live off one income only; and, even invest 10%-to-30% of the other spouse's income. Before you know it, neither spouse will have to work because you will be financially independent.

Always live below your means so you have excess income or cash flow to continue to invest in great businesses that continue to pay and raise their dividends each and every year.

IV. The Key to Door 3 – Take Advantage of the Greatest Opportunity to Come Around in Our Lifetime

Bitcoin has been around for about ten years. In May of 2010, Bitcoin was under 1-cent, got to 8-cents by July of 2010; and, its price has increased to about $19,000 per coin in 2017; it is now trading between $7,000 and $9,000 per coin. Bitcoin has created many multi-millionaires since its inception. However, some of the last ones to jump on the bandwagon have lost half of their investment.

In 2008, around the time of the financial crisis, a "white paper" was published by an individual known as Satoshi Nakamoto but, today, many people believe this was just a pen-name for a group of individuals. The "white paper" proposed a decentralized currency for individuals, "A purely peer-to-peer version of electronic cash [that] would allow online payments to be sent directly from one party to another without going through a financial institution."

Bitcoin functions because of blockchain technology. I'm not going to explain any of this because it takes too long, the information is readily available…just Google it, and, it is not relevant to what I am trying to convey here today. Many of you who have followed my DRIP recommendations and have invested in IBM, Microsoft, and yes, Wal-Mart, unbeknownst to you, are participating in this new blockchain technology already! You just won't have the possibility of turning a $250 stake into millions of dollars. Unless, of course, you take a position in several crypto-currencies!

Because of the success of Bitcoin, which exists because of blockchain technology, the last time I looked, there were 1,584 coins/tokens listed on CoinMarketCap.com (https://coinmarketcap.com/all/views/all/). Most of these crypto-currencies will not be successful.

Coinbase (https://www.coinbase.com/), for example, only currently allows the purchase and sale of Bitcoin, Bitcoin Cash, Ethereum, and Litecoin. I just read that they will be adding a fifth, ERC20 Ethereum Token.

One newsletter writer wrote, "Despite the hype and large paper profits, I was never comfortable recommending any of those early cryptos to readers. I'm still not... The early cryptocurrencies such as bitcoin (BTC), ether (ETH), litecoin (LTC) and ripple (XSP) are not worth serious consideration as stores of value with long-term potential for appreciation and profit."

Early Investing wrote a Report identifying "Five Digital Currencies That Will Overtake Bitcoin." You can access this Report at https://earlyinvesting.com/investing-research/digital-currencies/?code=X310T912&msclkid=50ee389773bb1ecee44e6228c38eb7ec by entering your email address. The Report explains why they believe these five crypto-currencies will overtake Bitcoin: (1) Ethereum (ETH); (2) Ripple (XRP); (3) Litecoin (LTC); (4) Dash (DASH); and (5) Monero (XMR). In spite of this Report, as of March 2018, they still had a position in Bitcoin, along with Ethereum, Litecoin, and New Economy Movement (XEM), which was not even mentioned. They did not have a position in Ripple, Dash or Monero? I bought Ripple (XRP) coins (https://ripple.com/) and the New Economy Movement (XEM) tokens.

There is a voluminous amount of information and hype about cryptocurrencies and many so-called experts willing to sell you an annual subscription to their crypto-currency newsletters for a going rate of $5,000; some offering first-time subscribers a discounted price of $3,000. Much of their information can be found by searching for yourself. For example, I searched for the Early Investing Report on the five digital currencies that will overtake Bitcoin and found a similar article from another source, which appeared to be identical. Coin Central (https://coincentral.com/) is a good source for information about crypto-currencies.

You may find our newsletter (www.jeffersoniangroup.com), which is currently free, at least through 2018, a great source for crypto-currency information, which you should personally verify yourself before taking a stake in a given coin or token. Keep reading and I'll show you the possibility of how you may be able to turn $250 into millions of dollars.

Let's just look at Bitcoin, which started out at about $0.08 and rose to a high of $19,000. Today it is trading over $7,000 per coin. If you had bought 1,000 Bitcoins for $0.25 per coin for a total cost of $250, you would have over $7,000,000 today. Hopefully, you would have sold 500 coins back when it reached $19,000 for a profit of $9,500,000 and, you would still have over $3,500,000 left in Bitcoins.

In my opinion, **the real money has already been made in Bitcoin**; it is older technology and there may be other opportunities that will turn a rather small stake of $250 into several million dollars. However, **there are no guarantees and you should be willing to lose your entire stake**.

The first coin I bought was **Stellar Lumens (XLM)** paying $0.25 per coin or $500.00 for 2,000 coins. This coin is supported by IBM and Deloitte (Big 4 International Public Accounting Firm). If you search for information on XLM, you will find many articles, plus they have their own website.

A. How I Bought Stellar Lumens (XLM)

Buying crypto-currencies is not that easy. However, there are many articles available which explain how to buy specific crypto-currencies. I did not use Coinbase for two reasons. First, I would have to buy either Bitcoin or Ethereum on Coinbase, then go to another exchange, like BINANCE (https://www.binance.com/) and trade my Bitcoin or Ethereum for XLM. The second reason I avoided Coinbase is that they turned information over to the IRS on 14,000 U.S. customers who had made trades of $20,000 or more from 2013 to 2015.

You cannot go directly to BINANCE unless you already have a crypto-currency because they do not accept U.S. Dollars, Euros, or any other fiat currencies. This may change in the future because this Hong Kong based exchange is moving to Malta.

Therefore, I went to KRAKEN (https://www.kraken.com/) because you can use U.S. dollars to buy over a dozen different crypto-currencies, including Stellar Lumens (XLM) and Ripple (XRP). I bought 2,000 XLM coins and 500 XRP coins. However, I strongly suggest you first acquire Stellar Lumens (XLM).

It is not that difficult to open an account with KRAKEN, but, you first must get verified; just follow the instructions. You will need your passport or driver's license, a recent utility bill with your name and address on it, and, you must be able to take a picture of your face, holding your identification on one side and a signed written statement on the other side of your face. My daughter took the picture of me on my Samsung Galaxy S7; the resolution on her iPhone was not acceptable.

Next, you must obtain the wiring instructions from your local branch bank, which would include the ABA number and Swift number, along with the relevant information for an intermediary bank, if applicable, and input that information; then the amount of money you want to wire transfer. This is not an ACH-type transfer, where you would input information from the bottom left corner of your check. You must use wire transfers to and from KRAKEN.

After you have been verified and entered your local bank account wiring instructions and the amount you want to wire to KRAKEN, they will provide you with the wire instructions to wire transfer the money from your local bank to your account at KRAKEN.

I wired $1,000.00 from my local branch at SunTrust Bank and spent about 1-hour there before all the paperwork was done. First, I had to open a new account under my name as it exactly was opened at KRAKEN, i.e., I had a joint account at SunTrust Bank. You also should do this for safety and security purposes, just keeping a minimum balance in the account to avoid paying fees; SunTrust requires $500 so I transferred $1,525 to cover this first transaction, $1,000 to KRAKEN and a $25 fee, leaving $500 in the account.

The next day the $1,000 showed up in my account at KRAKEN, they charged me $5 leaving $995 in U.S. Dollars. I then followed the instructions and bought 2,000 XLM coins and 500 XRP coins, leaving me with about $175 in cash on deposit at KRAKEN.

Unfortunately, the next coin I wanted to purchase, Cardano (ADA), is not available at KRAKEN. Therefore, I had to setup an account at BINANCE (https://www.binance.com/), which was very easy. Since BINANCE does not accept U.S. Dollars, I had to wire transfer more money from my SunTrust account to KRAKEN, then purchase enough Ethereum (ETH) to acquire the amount of Cardano (ADA) tokens and transfer the ETH to the wallet I setup in my BINANCE account. Then I traded the ETH for Cardano (ADA).

Since the crypto-currencies I have acquired to date represent less than $10,000, I am going to leave them there in the hot wallet created at KRAKEN and BINANCE. Ultimately, if things go as planned, I would liquidate some coins, by converting to cash and wiring the money back to SunTrust Bank; then I would transfer the remainder of the coins to my hardware wallet.

You should do your own research. Every crypto-currency I mentioned has its own website and there are plenty of articles on them. However, I strongly suggest you get an account setup at KRAKEN and buy Stellar Lumens (XLM) while it is under $0.50 per coin. You can wire transfer $300-to-$500 if that is all you feel comfortable doing right now.

If you have difficulty getting verified at KRAKEN or you already have an account at COINBASE, you can purchase enough Ethereum (ETH) using COINBASE, and, transfer ETH to BINANCE, which is also easier to setup.

Remember, you should only use money for these crypto-currencies that you feel comfortable losing. If you keep your commitment low, your upside is substantial, while your downside is minimal.

This is a once in a lifetime opportunity. Here's why. As previously discussed, Bitcoin started out at $0.08 per coin and rose to a high of $19,000 per coin. Let's just say we find a coin/token and we purchase 200 coins/tokens at $0.50 each for $100. If this coin/token increases in value to less than half of what Bitcoin achieved to date at $8,000, our 200 coins/tokens, costing $100, would be worth $1,600,000. Has this happened before and is it still possible... You Bet! Is it highly probable that we will select the right coins/tokens and turn such a small amount into a million dollars... Highly Unlikely... but, what do we really have to lose... think about all the money we waste each year on unnecessary things... carveout some of that money and take a chance that may never come around again in our lifetimes!

Let's just look at the one-year gains in 2017. If you had paid $1,000 at the beginning of the year for one of the following coins/tokens, here's what you would have earned by the end of the year:

1. Ripple (XRP) - $360,180
2. NEM (XEM) - $298,420
3. Ardor - $168,090
4. Stellar Lumens (XLM) - $144,410
5. Dash - $92,650
6. Ethereum (ETH) - $91,620
7. Golem - $84,340
8. Binance Coin - $80,610

9. Litecoin - $50,460
10. OmiseGo (OMG) - $33,150
11. Bitcoin - $13,180

As one commentator pointed out, Ripple (XRP) gained more in one year than Apple has in its entire existence. **This opportunity** to get in on the ground floor with a minimal financial commitment—money that you normally waste and can afford to lose—**just may turn out to be a very monumental success!?!**

"Nothing ventured, nothing gained." Ben Franklin

B. Tax Consequences of Speculating in Bitcoin and Other Crypto-Currencies

In IRS Notice 2014-21, the IRS has taken the position that "the sale or exchange of convertible virtual currency [e.g. Bitcoin], or the use of convertible virtual currency to pay for goods or services in a real-world economy transaction, has tax consequences that may result in a tax liability." Basically, the IRS has taken the position that every time a crypto-currency is sold or traded, or used to purchase goods or services, there is a tax consequence.

For most of you reading this newsletter, the purchase of any crypto-currency would most likely be treated as a capital asset, especially if you follow my recommendations. If you, for example, purchased Bitcoin over a year ago and sold half your position in December 2017, converting it to cash or U.S. dollars, you would have a long-term capital gain subject to a maximum capital gains tax of 20%. Likewise, if you exchanged your Bitcoin for other goods or services, you would still pay a capital gains tax on the value of those goods or services.

It appears that the IRS has taken the position that exchanging Bitcoin for another crypto-currency is also a taxable event, especially since the new tax law states that the Section 1031 Tax free Exchange provision only applies to real estate. However, even though the IRS may be taking the position that each exchange of a crypto-currency for another is a taxable event, if such a transaction was properly structured, I believe there is a position to avoid the U.S. capital gains tax until a crypto-currency is converted to cash, i.e., U.S. dollars or another fiat currency.

For example, if you wanted to buy Cardano (ADA), you would first have to buy Ethereum ((ETH) with U.S. dollars from an exchange like KRAKEN or COINBASE. Then you would exchange your ETH for ADA on the BINANCE exchange. Furthermore, as of this writing, you can only exchange crypto-currencies on BINANCE for other crypto-currencies, i.e., they do not accept U.S. dollars, Euros, or any other fiat currency. In my opinion, by using an exchange like BINANCE, and continuing to exchange one crypto-currency for another, you do not have a taxable event until you convert all or a portion of your holdings to cash or use some to purchase goods and services.

FinCEN, the Financial Crimes Enforcement Network, has also issued guidance on this issue (FIN-2013-G001, March 18, 2013). Tax fraud is considered money-laundering with a maximum penalty of $500,000 or twice the amount of money laundered, whichever is greater, plus up to 20 years in prison for each count. For example, if you converted Bitcoin to cash five times in 2017 and do not report these transactions and pay the requisite taxes, you could be threatened with a penalty of up to $2,500,000 and 100 years in prison. This is in addition to unpaid taxes, interest and penalties for not timely paying the required taxes.

Be careful, maintain a low profile, but, do not ignore the U.S. tax laws. Also, if you have a stake in crypto-currencies, do not prepare your own tax return. Hire a CPA or Tax Lawyer, and make sure they understand what you are doing. If you receive an "expert opinion" and follow it, even if it is later overturned by the Courts, you would avoid criminal prosecution.

C. Final Thoughts

Bitcoin has been the most successful speculative investment over the past decade; after all, it did rise from $0.08 to a high of $19,000. I've seen several predictions that Bitcoin will rise to $30,000 from its current price of just over $7,000. Another prognosticator wrote, "I predict Bitcoin will *still* hit $50,000 in 2018." They may be right but, I believe that other crypto-currencies offer a far greater opportunity going forward. In fact, the same person that believes that Bitcoin will hit $50,000 this year also recommends a dozen other crypto-currencies that he believes will increase in value much higher than Bitcoin right now.

Taking a small speculative position ($250-to-$1,000) in crypto-currencies is one of the few opportunities available to practically everyone. If you have more than $1-million in investment capital, $10,000, or less than 1% of your investment capital, is worth losing when compared to the potential upside.

I'm an optimist and hope to turn my $500 stake in 2,000 Stellar Lumens (XLM) coins into $3,800,000. If it hits $200,000, I will most likely sell half for $100,000, pay tax of $20,000, and invest the $80,000 in DRIP's. Hopefully the remaining 1,000 coins rise to $1,900 each worth $1,900,000!

Go to our website, Jeffersonian Group, LLC (www.jeffersoniangroup.com) and review our past Newsletters, which are free. We go into more detail on how to buy crypto-currencies and list our favorite coins/tokens.

V. The Key to Door 4 – Invest in DRIP's

With over 40-years working as a *Certified Public Accountant* helping people start and run businesses, protect their assets, plan for their retirement, and pass their estates to their children, grandchildren, and favorite charities, I have seen what works and what does not. Today, the typical investment advice received from brokers, money managers, and the financial planning community writ large, has not changed since I began my career in January 1976. Moreover, much of the curriculum to become a *Certified Financial Planner* has been prepared or highly influenced by the Insurance Industry and Wall Street. In other words, the two major industries that design and sell investment products are training financial planners to sell their products.

What is not recommended or even discussed are great businesses—that have survived recessions, depressions, and wars---that have dividend reinvestment programs (DRIP's) and have paid and raised their annual dividends for decades. Why would these DRIP's be ignored? Because Wall Street cannot make any money from them. And, the Securities and Exchange Commission (SEC), influenced by the power-brokers on Wall Street, have forbidden these companies from advertising their DRIP's. In addition, if an investor should stumble across these programs, the companies are required to send them a huge prospectus outlining all of the potential risks of their programs. These prospectuses are designed by and for attorneys and accountants (CPA's); and, both professionals—due to malpractice issues and not wanting to be blamed for any financial loses— will most likely discuss the disadvantages with you and recommend you contact your broker or financial planner for specific investment advice. Regardless of what you have been led to believe, the entire financial and legal system has been designed to benefit the Insurance Industry and Wall Street, not the typical investor, i.e. you and me.

The financial planning community never mentions the safest passive investment strategy available to attain and/or maintain financial independence. Many financial professionals, having been indoctrinated by the Insurance Industry and Wall Street, don't realize the benefits of such a strategy; and, if they did and recommended it to you, would only receive a one-time fee since you would not need their services anymore!

To easily attain financial independence without winning the lottery or receiving some other financial windfall (e.g., pick the next Bitcoin), **and, to maintain your financial freedom,** you should **invest in certain DRIP's** based upon their respective dividend yields at the time of purchase; and, their average annual percentage increases over 10 or more years. **If you follow the recommendations outlined in this book, you will not care if there is a stock market correction. You will look forward to stock market corrections** due to the fact your reinvested dividends buy more shares at lower prices; and, other great businesses become available for purchase because their dividend yields become higher as their prices fall.

It has been reported that someone asked Albert Einstein to name the greatest invention in human history and he simply replied, "compound interest." According to Einstein, "compound interest is the eighth wonder of the world. He who understands it, earns it ... he who doesn't ... pays it." By Investing in certain DRIP's, you are able to take advantage of Einstein's Law of Compound Interest.

For example, if you put $10,000 in a DRIP (dividend reinvestment program)[12] "yielding 5%--and the company grows its dividend 10%

---

[12] There are more than 1,000 stocks that offer dividend reinvestment programs and some companies actually offer discounts of up to 10% off the current market price if you buy direct from them. Information is available on a particular company's investor page or in their DRIP prospectus. Remember, just because a company offers a DRIP does not mean it is a good investment.

each year, so that in year number two you're earning 5.5%, in year number three you earn 6.05% and so on—you'll be sitting on well over $5 million at the end of 30 years. And this... doesn't even factor in the potential growth in share price!"[13]

As mentioned earlier, Grace Groner turned $180 into $7-million in 75-years through a DRIP with just one company; and, Anne Scheiber took a $5,000 investment in DRIP's and turned it into $22-million 51-years later.

And, according to professors Rubin and Spaht: "For those investors who adopt ten and fifteen-year horizons, [investing in certain DRIP's] will lead to financial independence for life."

Investing in certain DRIP's using the principle of compound interest is one simple approach to obtaining financial independence; and, in this uncertain world, certain DRIP's will allow you to maintain your financial freedom. We will show you how to find the right DRIP's, which ones to buy, and, when to buy them. It is really quite simple; even children can do it; and, you should encourage your children and grandchildren to do so!

Investing in a DRIP addresses two of the most pressing problems facing... you today: inflation and relentlessly low interest rates."[14] According to Dan Ferris, the ultimate stock strategy for any stock market correction or downturn "is buying the world's best businesses at great prices... and then compounding your way to wealth over many years." The businesses he is talking about have DRIP's and include "blue-chip *World Dominators* like Microsoft and Coca-Cola." "These businesses have tremendous advantages over their competitors. They generate huge cash flows, which are directed to shareholders in the form

---

[13] Addison Wiggins, *The Apogee Advisory*, Issue 20, November 2012 (Agora Financial, LLC).

[14] *Id.*

of higher dividends, share buybacks, and rising share prices." If you buy these businesses at great prices, "a stock market correction is nothing to worry about." "No matter what the day-to-day movements of the market are, World Dominator companies like Intel, Johnson & Johnson and Coca-Cola will still be No. 1 in their industries. They will still have giant, insurmountable competitive advantages. They'll still have consistently thick profit margins. They'll still generate huge cash flows. They'll still direct a portion of those cash flows to shareholders through ever-increasing dividends. And they will still allow shareholders to put the power of long-term wealth compounding to work."[15]

Remember, Grace Groner turned $180 into $7-million in 75-years through a DRIP with just one company; and, Anne Scheiber took a $5,000 investment in DRIP's and turned it into $22-million 51-years later.

The Coca-Cola Company (KO) has paid and raised its annual dividend each and every year for the past 55-years. Its name or brand is one of the most recognized throughout the world, selling its products in over 200 countries. If you had purchased 100 shares of KO on November 30, 1994 for $5,112 using the Company's DRIP or dividend reinvestment program, after 18 years ending December 17, 2012, your 100 shares would have grown to 1,958 shares worth $73,914 representing an average annual return per year of 74.56%. More importantly, the dividend yield, at the time of purchase was only 1.5% or $78. For the year ended December 17, 2012, that dividend payout to you would have grown to $1,977.44 representing a one-time yield or return on your original investment, just from the dividends received, for the year 2012 of 38.68%; this annual yield continues to increase each and every year. For the year ending December 15, 2016, the last quarterly dividend payment in 2016, the total dividends paid was $3,053.46 on this original investment

---

[15] Dan Ferris, *The Ultimate Stock Strategy for the Coming Correction*, Steve Sjuggerud's Daily Wealth Premium, Sept. 26, 2012.

of $5,112 representing a total return for 2016 of 59.73% based upon the dividend payments alone. And, within several more years, the annual dividend payments will exceed the original investment! **As DRIP investors, we do not care if the market crashes and the value of our KO shares drop because the dividend payout continues to increase each year; and, we are able to acquire more shares at less cost.**

The Coca-Cola Company (KO) example is an actual real-life purchase and the original purchase price would have been deemed too high because the dividend yield at the time of purchase was only 1.5%. In today's environment, you would be looking for dividend yields of at least 2.5% and higher before you would make a purchase. However, this is an excellent example of the benefits of long-term investing using the principle of compound interest, i.e., even if you pay more per share than is recommended for a great business that consistently pays and raises its dividend, over the long term, you will still end up receiving annual dividend payments greater than your original investment.

Keep reading. We will show you how and when to buy these great businesses, so your passive income or cash flow may increase much more quickly than the KO example above.

A. It's Never Too Late

Financial independence has nothing to do with retirement. Retirement is a new concept that arose during the 20th Century. For most of recorded history only royalty could feasibly retire. However, beginning about 1920 retirement became "feasible for the ordinary person." "Now those blissful days are gone. We're back to what's normal,"[16] at least for many people that rely solely on generous private pension plans that no longer exist and/or social security. But, here's the good news: According to Dr. David Eifrig, Jr., "too many people work and save all their lives only to

---

[16] Richard J. Maybury, *U.S. & World Early Warning Report*, July 2012.

retire and discover they are bored...literally to death. Many succumb to depression and disease (even terminal illness) because they are unprepared for the mental shift in retirement. In fact, a shocking study in 2005 showed people who retire at age 55 die twice as fast as those who keep working"[17] So, for those of you who have not accumulated investment capital that generates enough passive income to maintain the lifestyle you have become accustomed to, an early retirement would appear to be hazardous to your health.

Furthermore, many of us have family and friends who have lived and are living well into their 90's; and, the oldest verified living person was a French woman who passed away on August 4, 1997 at age 122 years, 164 days old. With the strides made and to be made in the future in medical science and technology, those of us in our 50's and 60's should plan on living at least another sixty (60) years or longer. Because of this, if we have not already attained financial independence, we will need to make better financial decisions going forward.

Colonel Harland David Sanders (1890 – 1980), at age 65, after his restaurant failed because of reduced customer traffic from the newly completed Interstate 75, took $105 from his first social security check and began visiting potential investors whom he thought may be interested in becoming franchisees. About nine years later he sold the Kentucky Fried Chicken corporation for $2-million to a partnership of Kentucky businessmen. This sale did not include his Canadian franchises. One year later he moved to Mississauga, Ontario to oversee his Canadian franchises; and, he continued to collect franchise and appearance fees in both Canada and in the United States. He also created several charitable trusts that to this day donate money to various groups that specialize in women's and children's care. Colonel Sanders was 90 years old when he passed away.

---

[17] David Eifrig, Jr., *The Retirement Millionaire Manifesto*, Retirement Millionaire Research Report, Stansberry & Associates.

The Colonel Sanders story illustrates several important lessons: **It is never too late; learn from your mistakes; never give up, adapt and prosper.** Also, this is an excellent example of turning a negative event, i.e., the failure of a business, into something much more beneficial. After all, there are no problems, only opportunities. Colonel Sanders took this negative event—the failure of his business—reevaluated his situation and made changes. The changes he made greatly improved his life and the lives of many others, who continue to benefit from his success.

Therefore, regardless of your age, your goal should be to obtain financial independence as soon as possible. Financial independence allows a person to work less or not at all, participate in more leisure activities, change careers, start new businesses, organize and contribute to charitable causes, etc. The quicker you become financially independent, the more freedom you have to do as you please.

B. How to Use DRIP's to Attain and Maintain Financial Freedom
   i. Why Invest in Specific Stocks That Pay Dividends?

Marc Lichtenfeld, author of *Get Rich With Dividends*, wrote the following, which comports with my experience:

> I was working on a dividend spreadsheet, changing the variables, when the size of the numbers I saw surprised me. I realized that if my kids' money was invested according to the formula I was working with, they should never have any financial problems in adulthood, no matter what job or career they choose.
>
> I also recognized that using the same formula, my wife and I should never have to worry about income in retirement.
>
> And last, I understood that if my parents invested according to the formula, they, too, should have no worries about income in old age.

[Investing in certain dividend-paying stocks (DRIP's)] is for the average investor—the investor who is just getting started and the investor who is playing catch-up, the investor who has been burned by the booms and busts of the recent past and the investor who trusted the wrong advisor and ended up paying thousands of dollars for worthless advice.

[This DRIP strategy] is for all investors who are serious about creating real wealth for themselves and their families, investors who are willing to learn a [very] simple system for making their money work as hard as they do (or did). It's easy to learn and implement and takes very little free time. Importantly, it's not a theory. It's been proved to work over decades of bull and bear markets.

And [**the DRIP investment strategy is] designed for investors who have other things they'd rather do than spend hours on their portfolios.**[18]

Dr. Jeremy Siegel, professor of finance at the prestigious Wharton School of Business, examined various asset classes for 210 years (1802

---

[18] Marc Lichtenfeld, *Get Rich With Dividends*, xvii, Second Edition, John Wiley & Sons, Inc. (2015). Bold emphasis added. This is an excellent book. Our approach is similar but different. We emphasize companies with international brands like Coca-Cola, McDonald's, Procter & Gamble, Johnson & Johnson, ExxonMobil, etc.; and, we like to emphasize Companies that pay and raise dividends for more than 25-years. In Lichtenfeld's *Compound Income Portfolio,* as of May 2017, the Companies he included have raised their annual dividends for an average of only 11.7 years. Our approach is more in-line with the research done by Professors Jeremy Siegel, Harvey Rubin and Carlos Spaht, II. In addition, Marc Lichtenfeld works for The Oxford Club, which sells many different newsletters and investment strategies. In order to keep his paying subscriber's, he may be more concerned with annual short-term gains. We are more concerned with acquiring great businesses that have paid and raised their dividends, on average, by 10% or more, for more than 25-years. Such companies have continued to raise and pay dividends through the 3-year Bear Market which began in 2000; and, continued to pay and raise dividends through the Great Recession that began in 2008.

through 2012) to include stocks, long & short term bonds, cash, and gold & commodities. Dr. Siegel concluded: "No other asset class—bonds, commodities, or the dollar—displays the stability of long-term real returns as do stocks."[19] Professor Siegel also determined: "Reinvesting dividends is the critical factor giving the edge to most winning stocks in the long run. In contrast to skeptics who claim that high-dividend paying firms lack "growth opportunities," the exact opposite is true." He also found that "the older, slower-growing firms [e.g., The Coca-Cola Company, ExxonMobil]" outperformed the fast-growing new firms, especially technology firms, over the long-run.[20]

Professor Siegel, through his extensive research, concluded: "Market cycles, although difficult on investors' psyches, generate wealth for long-term stockholders. These gains come not through timing the market but through reinvestment of dividends." According to Dr. Siegel, the additional shares acquired during market downturns act as a "bear-market protector," and the additional shares acquired turn into a "return accelerator" as prices rise again, as they always have.[21]

As a result of several studies, Louisiana State University professors Harvey Rubin and Carlos Spaht, II documented and concluded,

> the case for the long-term dividend investment strategy is strongly apparent. For those investors who adopt ten and fifteen-year horizons, the dividend investment strategy will lead to financial independence for life. Regardless of the direction of the market, a constant and growing dividend is a never-ending income stream.

---

[19] Jeremy J. Siegel, *Stocks For The Long Run*, 5-6, Fifth Edition, McGraw-Hill Education (2014).

[20] Jeremy J. Siegel, *The Future For Investors*, Kindle Edition, Crown Business (2005).

[21] *Id.*

> ...investments in high-quality, dividend-paying stocks can provide a safe and long-term plan for financial independence for those who have retired or will soon retire, and thereby negate the risk of outliving one's income.
>
> ...financial independence for life can be achieved with relatively small sums of money by making quality [DRIP] investments and being disciplined to do the same thing period after period of time.[22]

If you want to become financially independent—the ability to do what you want and when you want to do it, without having to work—you need to invest in certain great businesses that have a history of paying and raising their dividends. And, if you want to retire or are retired, and desire to not run out of money, you need to invest in certain great businesses that have a history of paying and raising their dividends. In addition, if you want to see your children and grandchildren avoid financial problems as adults, no matter what job or career they choose, you need to encourage them to invest in certain great businesses that have a history of paying and raising their dividends.

Based on over 40 years of experience as a Certified Public Accountant, Lawyer, and Business Consultant, helping my clients reduce taxes, protect assets, and plan for retirement, I have found that investing in certain DRIP's is the only safe and passive way to attain and maintain financial freedom.

---

[22] Harvey Rubin and Carlos Spaht, II, *Financial Independence Through Dollar Cost Averaging and Dividend Reinvestments*, Journal of Applied Business and Economics, vol. 12 (4) 2011.

ii. How to Select DRIP Stocks

At this time, there are 109 companies that are *U.S. Dividend Champions*, which are businesses that have paid and raised their annual dividends each and every year for at least 25-years. This list and the details necessary to determine which companies are great investments is available from The DRIP Investing Resource Center, http://www.dripinvesting.org/tools/tools.asp. Within this category are the *Dividend Aristocrats*, which are S&P 500 companies that have paid and raised their dividends for at least 25-years. This is the first category to look at for your basic portfolio, which may include up to a dozen or so stocks. There are two versions of this list. The first version is an Excel Spreadsheet, which you can download and save to your computer.

Unlike the Excel Spreadsheet, which includes only the *U.S. Dividend Champions*, the PDF Format includes the *U.S. Dividend Champions* plus two other lists: (1) *Contenders*, which are companies that have paid and raised their dividends for 10-to-24 years; and (2) the *Challengers*, which have paid and raised their dividends for 5-to-9 years.

It is recommended that you select companies that have a 2.5% or greater dividend yield at the time you purchase the stock; and, have a record of increasing their dividends by 8%-to-10% or more per year. The current price and dividend yield is usually available through your online discount broker or YAHOO! FINANCE (http://finance.yahoo.com/).

In the following pages, we will show you several dozen DRIP stocks that we picked from these lists and will explain why we selected them. In addition, you can access our past newsletters, which are free, at Jeffersonian Group, LLC (www.JeffersonianGroup.com). Also, if you have a particular question or concern, please go to Contact on our website and ask; we will attempt to answer you in our next newsletter.

iii. Basic Portfolio

In January of 2016, twelve DRIP stocks were selected that I believed should be in everyone's portfolio. The combined average dividend yield at the time of purchase was 3.03%; and, the combined average annual projected dividend increase was a conservatively computed 12.68%. Assuming no reinvestment of dividends, with this estimated annual increase in dividend payments, by year five the annual dividend yield would be about 5%; in eight years the dividend yield would be around 7%; in ten years the dividend yield would rise to over 9%; and, by the fifteenth year, the annual dividend yield would be over 16%. Also, by the fourteenth year, the total dividends received, which were not reinvested, would easily exceed the initial investment in these twelve stocks. Based upon history, these annual dividend increases should occur even when the stock market crashes.

One of the DRIP stocks in this recommended basic portfolio is The Coca-Cola Company (KO), which has paid and raised dividends each and every year for the past 55-years. Over the past 17-years, KO has raised its annual dividend, on average, by 9.1%., which is the percentage used for KO to compute the percentage increase in the combined portfolio of the twelve DRIP stocks that are included in the basic portfolio. In addition, the dividend yield in January 2016 for KO was 3.14% based upon the purchase price; this was the yield when the stock was purchased.

But, **by reinvesting the dividends, which takes advantage of the principle of compound interest, the average annual dividend increase is dramatically higher**. For example, when 100 shares of KO was acquired in November 1994 for a cost of $5,112, the annual dividend was $78 representing a dividend yield of 1.53%, about 50% less than the beginning yield of the basic portfolio. After reinvesting dividends, eight years later the annual dividend grew from $78.00 to $597.63, representing an annual dividend yield of 11.69%; by the tenth year, the dividends paid was $775.67

which amounted to a 15.17% dividend yield; and, by the fourteenth year, the original 100 shares grew to 676.655 shares paying $1,307.43 in annual dividends, representing a 25.58% annual dividend yield.

The following chart compares the growth of annual dividends with no reinvestment; and, with reinvested dividends, which takes advantage of the principle of compound interest:

	Basic Portfolio No Reinvestment (Estimated)	Coca-Cola Reinvested Dividends (Actual)
Date of Purchase	3.03%	1.53%
Eight Years	7.00%	11.69%
Ten Years	9.00%	15.17%
15-Years & 14-Years	16.00%	25.58%

As illustrated above, by reinvesting dividends, even when you start out with about half the yield, e.g., 1.53% versus 3.03% and, the average annual increase appears less (9.1% rather than 12.68%), the actual annual dividend yield is remarkably greater. This substantial increase is due to the principle of compound interest. Therefore, by reinvesting your dividends, you can still acquire stocks with less than a 2.5% yield on the date of acquisition, but, you still need to make sure that they have a history of paying and raising their dividends by at least 8%-to-10% per year.

The *Basic Portfolio* follows:

U.S. Dividend Champions/Dividend Aristocrats—S&P 500—Paid/Raised Over 25-Years

1. AFLAC, Inc. (AFL) - $57.47; 2.86% Yield; 34-Years; 15.9% Avg. Incr.

2. Coca-Cola Company (KO) - $42.42; Yield 3.14%; 55-Years; 9.1% Avg. Incr.
3. Colgate-Palmolive Co. (CL) - $64.54; Yield 2.35%; 54-Years; 10.4% Avg. Incr.
4. ExxonMobil Corp. (XOM) - $75.33; Yield 3.81%; 35-Years; 7.8% Avg. Incr.
5. Johnson & Johnson (JNJ) - $98.86; Yield 3.10%; 55-Years; 10.9% Avg. Incr.
6. McDonald's Corp. (MCD) - $120.50; Yield 3.01%; 41-Years; 20.1% Avg. Incr.
7. Procter & Gamble (PG) - $79.10; Yield 3.43%; 61-Years; 9.0% Avg. Incr.
8. Sysco Corp. (SYY) - $39.39; Yield 3.13%; 47-Years; 11.6% Avg. Incr.
9. Wal-Mart Stores, Inc. (WMT) - $64.38; Yield 3.13%; 44-Years, 14.8% Avg. Incr.

Contenders (Paid & Raised Dividends for 10-to-24 Straight Years)

10. Microsoft Corp. (MSFT) - $52.36; Yield 2.75%; 15-Years; 14.8% Avg. Incr.

Other Great Businesses

11. Intel Corporation (INTC) - $29.96; Yield 3.21%; Paid Dividends 24-Years
12. Walt Disney Company (DIS) - $95.87; Yield 1.47%; Paid Dividends 36-Years

The reason you want your *Basic Portfolio* to include *World Dominating* businesses that have paid and raised their dividends for 25-years and longer is because these companies have continued to raise their dividends during stock market crashes; and, the Great Recession and stock market crash of 2008. In fact, the current 109 *U.S. Dividend*

Champions continued to pay and raise their annual dividends through the stock market crash that began in 2000 and lasted for 3-years through 2002; and, they continued to pay and raise their dividends through the Great Recession and stock market crash that began in 2008, which was considered the worst recession since the depression that began in 1929.

Therefore, you may prefer to limit your *Basic Portfolio* to *U.S. Dividend Champions* rather than include the three other companies (MSFT, INTC and DIS) identified above. Keep reading and you'll find out why these three great businesses are included in my *Basic Portfolio*.

Unfortunately, most large corporations tend to get bad press, including several of my selections. Politicians constantly bad-mouth certain companies, especially during campaigns, stating that they do not pay their fair share of taxes and/or they don't pay their employees enough. This is a fraud perpetrated against all of us. First, corporations do not pay taxes; they only collect taxes. Only individuals, not inanimate objects, pay taxes. When a tax is levied on a corporation, it is either: (1) Paid by the employees, through reduced salary increases, elimination of bonuses, or a reduction in hiring; (2) by the shareholders through a reduction in dividend payments or shareholder value; and, (3) the tax is ultimately included in the price of the products or services provided by the companies. In other words, it is everyone, especially the poor and middle-class, that ultimately pays corporate income taxes and all other taxes, which are included in the cost of the products and services they use. Corporations are not evil; the political hacks that vilify and tax them are the evil-doers! Corporations provide jobs. And, they provide the products and services we demand to make our lives better. By investing in these great businesses, you are keeping the American Dream alive; and, getting closer to financial independence or maintaining your financial freedom.

Let's now look at some of my selections. ExxonMobil, McDonald's,

Wal-Mart, and even Coca-Cola tend to get a bad-rap from the press from-time-to-time; and, you may not like one or all of these great businesses. But, whether or not you agree with my rationale, you have to love their business plans and how good they treat their shareholders, hopefully, you in the future, and me right now!

Why would you buy these businesses, especially if you don't really like them? Let's look at ExxonMobil, the big bad oil company, an undeserved reputation. ExxonMobil has paid dividends for 118 years straight and is one of the world's largest employers creating opportunities for employment worldwide. In addition, this is an energy company, not just an oil company. When alternative energies become efficient and profitable, it is ExxonMobil, Chevron, and Shell that will either develop that technology or purchase it. If you want to be on the forefront of energy technology and get paid while you wait, this is the company to buy right now. Also, if you have any family or friends that want to enter the field of engineering, they should consider opportunities at these three energy companies; with a BS in Engineering, a starting salary in excess of $120,000 is not unusual. And finally, I still put gasoline in my auto, so I obviously stop at ExxonMobil gas stations; as I'm pumping the gas, I feel like I am paying myself!

No company can touch McDonald's; it has over 35,000 restaurants worldwide in 118 countries, with 1.7 million employees, serving 68 million customers daily. When McDonald's adds an ingredient to its menu, it instantly becomes one of the world's largest purchasers for that ingredient. It took McDonald's two years to coordinate enough cucumbers to launch its McWrap sandwich nationwide. They sell sushi in Japan, angus beef in Sweden, and now kale breakfast bowls in Southern California. Not to mention that McDonald's has paid and raised its dividend for 41 straight years by an average of 20.1% over the past 17-years. You may not like their food, but, you gotta love their business model and how they treat their stockholders. Have you tried their breakfast meals and coffee recently? Their fancy coffees are as good as Starbucks and a lot cheaper! And, when you are on-the-road, they consistently have the cleanest bathrooms...just saying...

As of January 31, 2017, Wal-Mart had 11,695 stores and clubs in 28 countries. Wal-Mart is the World's largest company by revenue, with approximately $480-billion in 2016; and, is the World's largest private employer with 2.3-million employees worldwide; about 1.5-million people are employed in the United States. Several days before writing this, I had heard a financial commentator say that Wal-Mart was getting into online shopping big-time and is challenging Amazon.com; he predicted that Wal-Mart would ultimately beat-out Amazon.com. I take my grandchildren to Wal-Mart because they love going up and down the toy aisles. I'll purchase some wrangler jeans, Coca-Cola products (e.g., Dasani water) and Procter & Gamble products at Wal-Mart because I own the stock and they treat their stockholders with respect by paying and raising their dividends for the past 44-years!

The Coca-Cola Company (KO) is one of the most recognized brand names in the world. KO has over 500 sparkling and still brands selling 1.9-billion servings per day in over 200 countries. When Coca-Cola sales flattened in the United States, they concentrated on still brands with a healthier perspective. For example, Dasani and Glaceau Smart Water are two of the four top-selling still water brands in the United States, which are owned by KO. Dasani was number 1 in 2016 with 1.07-billion U.S. dollars in sales. This is a great company that everyone should own!

The other five *U.S. Dividend Champions/Aristocrats* have great stories and histories but, I'll leave that to you to explore. However, **the only true measure that you really have to understand is this: These great businesses have paid and raised their annual dividends for at least 25-years straight; and, they have a history of increasing their annual dividends by 8%-to-10% and more.**

Why stray from the *U.S. Dividend Champions/Aristocrats*? Why Microsoft? Dan Ferris once described Microsoft Corporation (MSFT) as a *World Dominating Dividend Grower*. I've been using Microsoft products for as long as I can remember and I like to own stocks of companies whose products I use. Since Microsoft is the world's largest developer of software with a staff of 118,000 employees working in 100 countries, Dan Ferris appears to have been right since Microsoft has also paid and raised its dividends by 14.8%, on average, over the past 15-years. According to Value Line Select, *Dividend Income & Growth Service*, Microsoft "produces over $22 billion in net profits, on $92 billion in revenues, a year." Furthermore, management is "building up business in the lucrative cloud computing & storage and mobile services areas." This investment service of Value Line recommended Microsoft in August 2016. With a dividend yield above 2.5%, Microsoft was included in my *Basic Portfolio* back in January 2016.

Intel Corporation (INTC) is a similar story in that every computer I have ever owned has had Intel's core processor inside them. Intel has paid a dividend for 24-years straight but, has only started to regularly raise their annual dividends. Another source that you can use to determine the dividend status of a particular company is Dividata, LLC, https://www.dividata.com/, which gives an Overall Rating of Above Average (4) for Intel Corporation and gives it an Excellent (5) rating for Dividend History and Stability. I own Intel Corporation but, you should consider purchasing it only after you have acquired all of the nine *U.S. Dividend Champions/Aristocrats* and Microsoft, the *Contender*.

The Walt Disney Company (DIS) has a special place in my heart. We moved to Florida when our daughter was 4 years old and we had a son 5 years later. Disney World offers Florida Residents great deals on annual passes, so we spent quite a bit of time in Disney World while our children were growing up. Now, with two grandchildren, we started back again! Also, and more importantly, I had bought Disney stock back in January 1986 after having been to Disney World numerous times from August 1983 when we first moved to Florida. Due to stock-splits alone,100 shares purchased in January 1986 for $11,262 grew to 4,800 shares 30 years later worth $480,600 in 2015. Disney is a *World Dominator*, the world's largest media business, which owns Star Wars, Marvel, ESPN, ABC, The A&E Network, a cruise line, a global network of resorts, Touchtone, and Pixar. In the January Issue of *Sure Dividend* by Ben Reynolds, Disney (DIS) was one of his top ten dividend stocks. I've owned Disney stock since 1986 and have purchased more shares over the last several years. In addition, I am buying shares for my two grandchildren. Disney is a *World Dominating* Great Business that has not decreased its dividend payout for 33 straight years; and, historically tended to split its stock on a fairly regular basis. Disney's yield is always less than 2% but, this is the one exception I have— to the 2.5% or better yield rule— because Disney has an historical record of consistent stock-splits over the long term.

iv. Other U.S. Dividend Champions to Consider

In our June 2017 newsletter, Issue 14-2017, four of the twelve stocks in the *Basic Portfolio* had risen in value dropping the dividend yield below our recommended entry yield of 2.5% or greater. Therefore, we recommended other *U.S. Dividend Champions*, that were also *Dividend Aristocrats* that had yields greater than 2.5%. You may want to consider the following great businesses for your portfolio:

1. Archer Daniels Midland (ADM) - $42.45; Yield 3.02%; 42-Years; Avg. Incr. 12.2%
2. Kimberly-Clark Corp. (KMB) - $129.51; Yield 3.00%; 45-Years; Avg. Incr. 8%
3. PepsiCo, Inc. (PEP) - $117.91; Yield 2.73%; 44-Years; Avg. Incr. 10.8%
4. Target Corp. (TGT) - $54.40; Yield 4.41%; 49-Years; Avg. Incr. 15.7%

5. VF Corp. (VFC) - $53.71; Yield 3.13%; 44-Years; Avg. Incr. 13.3%
6. Weyco Group, Inc. (WEYS) - $27.29; Yield 3.22%; 35-Years; Avg. Incr. 12%

With respect to *U.S. Dividend Champions/Aristocrats*, the only important criteria is the yield of 2.5% or greater when you acquire the stock; and, you only acquire the stock if the historical average annual dividend increase has been 8%-to-10% or greater.

A word of caution, with Amazon.com and online shopping, the big retailers like Target and Wal-Mart, may experience difficulties. Therefore, if they stop increasing their annual dividends, it may be time to sell. However, as of this writing, I believe Wal-Mart will hold its own, while Target may have some difficulties. If you are concerned, avoid Target at this time.

If you go to Jeffersonian Group, LLC (www.JeffersonianGroup.com), our past newsletters are available to you at no cost. Much of the information is still current and may be useful to you.

v. Contenders Worthy of Consideration

In our June 2017 newsletter, we also identified six *Contenders*—companies that have paid and raised their dividends for 10-to-24 years straight—that we believed were priced right for acquisition:

1. Enterprise Products Partners (EPD) - $26.89; Yield 6.17%; 20-Years; Avg. Incr. 5.9%
2. General Mills (GIS) - $57.32; Yield 3.35%; 13-Years; Avg. Incr. 10.4%
3. Int'l Business Machines (IBM) - $152.49; Yield 3.93%; 21-Years; Avg. Incr. 17.5%
4. Lockheed Martin (LMT) - $283.65; Yield 2.57%; 14-Years; Avg. Incr. 18.4%

5. Omega Healthcare Investors (OHI) - $31.56; Yield 7.98%; 15-Years; Avg. Incr. 9.4%
6. Qualcomm Inc. (QCOM) - $57.52; Yield 3.96%; 14-Years; Avg. Incr. 16.5%

Enterprise Products Partners (EPD) average annual increase in its annual dividend is less than 8% but, its' yield is almost two and one-half times greater than the entry point of 2.5%! There are always exceptions to the rule, but, you may feel more comfortable sticking to the rules as you put your portfolio together.

Our free newsletters are available at www.JeffersonianGroup.com, which will provide you with more information about this investment strategy, not normally recommended by the financial planning community; most likely due to lack of understanding and indoctrination by Wall Street and the Insurance Industry. Or, is it because of greed?

vi. Challengers You May Want to Consider

Challengers are companies that have paid and raised their dividends for 5-to-9 years straight. We identified two that we liked in our June 2017 newsletter available at www.JeffersonianGroup.com:

- AbbVie Inc. (ABBV) - $66.06; Yield 3.88%; 5-Years; Avg. Incr. 12.5%
- Cisco Systems Inc. (CSCO) - $31.50; Yield 3.68%; 7-Years; Avg. Incr. 40.6%

AbbVie Inc. (ABBV) was created in January 2013 as a spin-off from Abbot Laboratories, which has paid dividends for 45-years. ABBV has paid dividends since it was created and its most recent increase was 12.8%. ABBV was liked and recommended by Marc Lichtenfeld, who wrote *Get Rich With Dividends* and Ben Reynolds, *Sure Dividend* (January 2017 Edition).

Cisco Systems has raised its dividend on average by 40.6% over the past five years; and, Marc Lichenfeld included it in his *Compound Income Portfolio*. The Oxford Income Letter, Issue 50, May 2017.

Again, you should first concentrate on *U.S. Dividend Champions/ Aristocrats* when building your portfolio.

And finally, you may access our past newsletters, which are free through 2018, to see the new additions we add on a regular basis; visit us at Jeffersonian Group, LLC (www.JeffersonianGroup.com).

vii. How to Begin Investing

We have included 26 companies that paid and raised their dividends which we believed were good buys at the time we had originally recommended them. By the time you read this, some of these companies may be overpriced based upon the recommended yield of 2.5% or greater. If they are over-priced, you should avoid the over-priced companies until they come down in value.

On the other hand, the market may have crashed and it is quite possible that all of these companies have yields much greater than 2.5%. If that is the case, all of these 26 companies may be great buys by the time you read this. In addition, as of this writing there were 109 *U.S. Dividend Champions* and fifty of them were *Dividend Aristocrats*. If the stock market has crashed as you are reading this, you should take another look at the other *Dividend Aristocrats* not included within these pages. Who knows, you may find some great buys with companies that you may like much better than the ones identified above. In addition, you may follow us to see what we are currently doing at www.JeffersonianGroup.com.

Also, some of you may have $100,000 or more to invest and some of you may only have $1,000. Using a discount broker (e.g., E*TRADE, Charles Schwab, TD Ameritrade, Fidelity, etc.), you can now buy 10 shares or 1,000 shares and the brokerage fees will be less than ten dollars. In addition, once you acquire any of these DRIP stocks, you can instruct your broker to automatically reinvest the dividends at no cost.

If you only have $1,000 to invest, buy 20 shares of Coca-Cola (KO); then buy more shares next month; or, pick any other *U.S. Dividend Champion/Aristocrat* that you personally like that has a yield of at least 2.5%; and, has paid and raised its annual dividend, on average, by 8%-to-10% or more each year.

As an alternative, you might select one-to-three stocks to acquire each month. Do whatever you feel comfortable with, just start investing in these great businesses. If you have a substantial nest-egg to immediately invest in DRIP's, it is suggested that you invest 75% of it in DRIP's over a 3-to-6-month period.

Remember, the only way to become financially independent is to acquire assets (e.g., *U.S. Dividend Champion* DRIP's) that pay you passive income that exceeds your lifestyle expenses.

viii. Diversification Myths and What Not to Buy

Diversification is always touted as a necessity by Wall Street and financial planners. They hope that by spreading your risk around, should one asset class do poorly, another asset class will do well enough so your overall annual return on your **speculation** will, hopefully, be positive; or, at least, less negative than the broader market indexes.

Notice the term I used was **speculation** and not investment. **If you purchase mutual funds, ETF's, gold & precious metals, commodities, options, currency contracts, real estate, and whatever other financial product offered by Wall Street, you are not investing, you are speculating, i.e., you are hoping that in the future, someone else will come along and pay you more than what you paid for that**

particular asset. This approach is commonly referred to as the greater fool theory, i.e., you are looking for the "greater fool" who is willing to pay you more than you paid for the same asset. Sometimes it works and sometimes it doesn't.

The late Harry Browne came up with an investment strategy that he named, *The Permanent Portfolio*. There is a mutual fund designed to follow his approach, Permanent Portfolio Fund (PRPFX). He believed that by putting 25% in Stocks, 25% in Bonds, 25% in Gold and 25% in Cash, your investment would grow each and every year with very little downside risk. The premise was that if one sector crashed (e.g., Stocks), the other three investment categories representing 75% of the assets, would rise and cover the losses. You would then rebalance your fund or portfolio when an asset category got down to 15% or became greater than 35% based upon market fluctuations. This strategy seemed to work reasonably well during inflationary periods before interest rates dropped significantly. Richard Maybury, *Early Warning Report*, was a big proponent of the *Permanent Portfolio Fund*. In August 2015 he wrote, "With great reluctance, I have decided to drop the **Permanent Portfolio Fund (PRPFX)** from our recommendations. For more than thirty years I have recommended Harry Browne's Permanent Portfolio and Variable Portfolio strategy ... But now I'm afraid it is obsolete."[23] He is absolutely right, Harry Browne's investment strategy "is obsolete."

Therefore, **do not buy mutual funds of any type**, including Index Funds and ETF's that are made up of dividend-paying stocks, including all of the *Dividend Aristocrats*. Not all *Dividend Aristocrats* are great investments and you still pay fees. You are significantly better-off buying the individual stocks yourself.

---

[23] Richard J. Maybury, *Early Warning Report*, August 2015. I subscribe to Maybury's newsletter and respect most of his opinions but, he appears to have no idea that DRIP's exist.

Do not buy bonds. There is no upside and they will not keep up with inflation. Furthermore, you have risk of principal and your returns are abysmal, i.e., the low returns do not justify the risk. Finally, interest rates have been artificially held down for far too long and will ultimately have to rise. When they rise, every increase in the interest rate represents a decrease in principal value. As a rule of thumb, with respect to bonds, if interest rates rise by 1% the principal value of your bond will drop by 10% or more.

Do not buy real estate or vacant land for investment unless you want to actively be in business and/or can do most of the work yourself. Any cash flow gained in the short-term may be needed for repairs, improvements, and fees necessary to evict bad-tenants. Vacant land, unless it is farmable, normally does not generate any income, only costs for taxes and insurance. In addition, we now have environmental concerns and government regulations to deal with. Furthermore, most people will not be able to diversify enough to avoid risk. For example, if you invest on your own or through a limited partnership, which purchases a building and leases it back to Walgreens, this sounds like a safe investment. However, if the Walgreens is located in a major city and it is burned to the ground because of riots and demonstrations similar to what happened in Ferguson, Missouri and Baltimore, Maryland, you would have lost your entire investment. A better option would have been to invest in the DRIP offered by Walgreens Boots Alliance (WBA), with stores all over the United States and throughout Europe, which has paid dividends for 41 years; and, raised their annual dividend payments for over 25 years straight.

Do not buy gold for investment, it pays nothing. This is truly a speculation. Gold prices soar every so often but the prices always collapse. Furthermore, it is being sold as an ultimate replacement for the U.S. Dollar and other paper currencies. Unfortunately, if we reach the point where gold is necessary to act as a medium of exchange and all the great businesses of the world (e.g., Coca-Cola, Johnson & Johnson, Proctor

& Gamble, etc.) collapse, the most valuable investments to have would be guns & ammo, the ability to raise & grow your own food, and access to a water supply.

Buy gold and silver coins for their beauty and collectability and only if you have already obtained financial independence; or, have a great cash flow and your gold and silver acquisitions would not significantly delay your goal of obtaining financial independence.

In today's environment, the only safe investment—OUR DRIP STRATEGY— is to buy great businesses with worldwide operations, that have survived wars, recessions, and depressions; and, have paid and raised dividends for at least 10-to-25 years and longer. Anything else, e.g., mutual funds, is a pure speculation. As of this writing, there are 109 *U.S. Dividend Champions* and within this category are 50 *Dividend Aristocrats*, which have paid and raised their dividends annually for at least 25 years.

It is recommended that you purchase companies that pay at least a 2.5% or better dividend at the time of your purchase; and, that pay and raise their annual dividends by 8%-to-10% or more per year. The current price and dividend yield is usually available through your online discount broker or YAHOO! FINANCE (http://finance.yahoo.com/).

Diversification is overblown. If you invest in companies with worldwide operations, like the *Dividend Aristocrats* (e.g., Coca-Cola, Johnson & Johnson, Procter & Gamble, ExxonMobil, etc.), you are diversified throughout the world. In effect, you are not putting all of your eggs in one basket. By investing in twelve *Dividend Aristocrats*, you have your eggs in twelve different baskets! If these companies implode, we are all in real trouble; and, your best assets would not be gold & precious metals— making you a target of the less fortunate—it would be guns & ammo, access to a water supply, and the ability to feed yourself and your family.

VI. Wrapping It All Up

If you think about it, the only way you are able to enjoy freedom is if you are free to make decisions and act on the basis of your choices. Did you actually choose to work 40-hours per week for most of your life? Are you satisfied with weekends off and 2-to-4 week vacations per year? Some of you may be thinking, I wish I was that lucky, i.e., I wish I had weekends off and a 4-week vacation every year!

To achieve financial freedom, you must acquire assets that pay you passive income that continues to grow and always exceeds your expenses necessary to maintain your lifestyle. It is not so much about how much money you make, it has much more to do with how you spend your money. If you receive a $5,000 bonus, do you buy a Jet Ski or 100 shares of The Coca-Cola Company (KO)? The decision to purchase 100 shares of KO puts you on the fast-path to financial independence. If the Jet Ski is more important, you will most likely be subject to the whims of your employer or customers/clients for most of your life; in effect, you are a slave to your employer or customers/clients and to the government, which takes a significant portion of your daily earnings in the form of Income Taxes, Social Security & Medicare Taxes. If you continue to "keep up with the Jones' and opt for the Jet Ski, a bigger home, new furniture, new luxury automobiles,[24] a vacation home, a boat or yacht, country club memberships, ad infinitum, you may never throw-off your chains.[25] The choice is yours... Financial Freedom or Economic Slavery?

To attain and/or maintain financial freedom, the absolute best investments

---

[24] If you want a luxury automobile, buy one that is at least 2-years old. They are half the price and still come with a warranty! Invest the difference in DRIP stocks!

[25] You can have that bigger home or boat or whatever, just wait until your passive income increases enough to pay for it.

to acquire—which utilizes the principal of compound interest—are the stocks of great "slower-growing" businesses—that have survived wars, recessions and depressions—that have a history of paying and raising their dividends each and every year for 25-years and longer; companies like The Coca-Cola Company, ExxonMobil, Johnson & Johnson, Procter & Gamble, McDonald's, and a bountiful basket of other diverse *U.S. Dividend Champions/Aristocrats*.

Professors Rubin and Spaht concluded, "For those investors who adopt ten and fifteen year horizons, the dividend investment strategy will lead to financial independence for life. Regardless of the direction of the market, a constant and growing dividend is a never-ending income stream."

Therefore, if you want to become financially independent—the ability to do what you want and when you want to do it, without having to work—you need to invest in certain great businesses that have a history of paying and raising their dividends. And, if you want to retire or are retired, and desire to not run out of money, you need to invest in certain great businesses that have a history of paying and raising their dividends. In addition, if you want to see your children and grandchildren avoid financial problems as adults, no matter what job or career they choose, you need to encourage them to invest in certain great businesses that have a history of paying and raising their dividends.

Based on over 40 years of experience as a Certified Public Accountant, Lawyer, and Business Consultant, helping my clients reduce taxes, protect assets, and plan for retirement, I have found that investing in certain DRIP's is the only safe and passive way to attain and maintain financial freedom.

The aim of this book is to change your paradigm, developed after so many years of indoctrination and continued propaganda leveled at you by Wall Street, the Insurance Industry, and the entire financial planning community. If you have been convinced to start investing using our

DRIP strategy, you will be on your way to attaining financial independence, maintaining your financial freedom; and, you will not run out of money.[26]

Finally, do not forget to earmark at least $1,000, or no more than you can afford to lose, to crypto-currencies, the greatest opportunity to come around in our lifetimes, which is currently available to practically everyone!

Investing in DRIP's as explained above will secure your future. Not so with crypto-currencies, but, the upside is substantial, while the downside is limited to what each of us feel comfortable losing. Good luck to us all!

Dum Spiro, spero—While I breathe I hope.

Slainte mhath,

Robert G. Beard, Jr.

PS: Our past newsletters are available for free on our website; and, you can see which DRIPs are currently included in our portfolios, along with a listing of our favorite crypto-currencies. In addition, if you have any questions, please contact us; we will attempt to answer your questions in future newsletters. Our website is www.JeffersonianGroup.com.

---

[26] Don't forget, you must live below your means, so you can continue to regularly invest in certain DRIPs, as outlined in this book.

About the Author

Robert G. Beard Jr. is a Certified Public Accountant and holds a B.S. in Business Administration, a Juris Doctor (J.D.) and Master of Laws (LL.M.) in International Taxation and Financial Services. Along with his LL.M., he received a Certificate of Expertise in Anti-Money Laundering & Compliance, summa cum laude. He has worked for three of the four largest international public accounting firms and has over 40 years of experience in accounting, taxation, estate & asset protection, financial and business planning. Bob is also a Vietnam Era Veteran with an Honorable Discharge from the United States Air Force.

Other Publications

- The Best Kept Secret to Financial Freedom

- The U.S. Individual Income Tax is Incompatible with a Free Society

- How to Prepare For, Control, and Successfully Survive an IRS Audit

- Our Right to Privacy Hijacked by Government

- The United States Government is Illegitimate

www.ingramcontent.com/pod-product-compliance
Lightning Source LLC
Chambersburg PA
CBHW030509220526
45464CB00006B/2718